JOURNAL OF A TRIP TO CALIFORNIA: ACROSS THE CONTINENT FROM WESTON, MO., TO WEBER CREEK, CAL., IN THE SUMMER OF 1850

BY

Charles W. Smith

JOURNAL OF A TRIP TO CALIFORNIA: ACROSS THE CONTINENT FROM WESTON, MO., TO WEBER CREEK, CAL., IN THE SUMMER OF 1850

Published by Firework Press

New York City, NY

First published circa 2016

Copyright © Firework Press, 2015

All rights reserved

Except in the United States of America, this book is sold subject to the condition that it shall not, by way of trade or otherwise, be lent, re-sold, hired out, or otherwise circulated without the publisher's prior consent in any form of binding or cover other than that in which it is published and without a similar condition including this condition being imposed on the subsequent purchaser.

ABOUT FIREWORK PRESS

Firework Press prints and publishes the greatest books about American history ever written, including seminal works written by our nation's most influential figures.

INTRODUCTION.

Several years ago I had the good fortune to find, in the lumber and rubbish of a storeroom, this little journal. A small leather-backed notebook, it had lain unnoticed and forgotten for more than half a century in the author's old homestead.

The original manuscript is written in a 4 by 6-inch notebook, bound in boards. It contains 180 pages of text, with pressed western flowers and plants pasted on the five fly-leaves at the end.

Mr. William Smith, our author's father, came from Gloucestershire, England, in 1831 and settled on a farm (now owned by his grandson, George Smith) just west of the village of Victor, N. Y. For several years Mr. Smith's sons, James and Charles W., both helped him on the farm, but eventually the latter decided to become a printer and so obtained a position in the neighboring village of Canandaigua.

At the time of the discovery of gold in California, Mr. C. W. Smith had been for several years on the staff of the Ontario Messenger, which perhaps accounts for the interesting and newsy style in which his journal is written. Certain it is that he showed more than usual ability and training in narrating the experiences of the overland journey and especially in painting a vivid picture of the prairies, the rivers and mountains, the rocks and the flowers.

And so the Spring of 1850 found Mr. Smith leaving his place in the composing room at Canandaigua and, after a brief farewell visit with his family in Victor, he proceeded to Centreville, Indiana, from which town he dated the first entry of his narrative. The journal itself tells the rest of the story, and I am sure that the student of western history will find it one of the most valuable of the contemporary journals of the Forty-Niners and the Overland Trail.

R. W. G. Vail.

The Minnesota Historical Society, March 20, 1920.

FOOTNOTE:

A portrait of the author, painted in East Bloomfield, N. Y., is still owned by the family in Victor.—ED.

LETTER TO MOTHER.

April 10, 1853.
Dear Mother:

I have concluded to send you my journal, not because I think it contains anything of great interest, but because I know you will take it as an evidence that I have not forgotten my Mother.

Nancy and I have been married two years today, and through that time have walked peacefully along the path of life together, a path on which little Alice now presses her tiny feet and, holding a little hand in each of ours, will make our union more complete. It is now nearly six years since I left home, a home which I then expected to see again in a few months, and would have seen had I been able to return in a better condition than when I left it, for it is always expected that when a young man goes out upon the world, it is to rise and prosper, and not return in rags. And if it was not for that ambitious feeling that forbids there are now thousands in California and Oregon, who would instantly start for those good old homes on the other side of the Rocky Mountains. In all my wanderings I have been singularly fortunate, always having my health, and never meeting with those accidents which are common to persons in an unsettled condition. In regard to the good things of this world, I have reason to be grateful, rather however for what we expect, than what we now enjoy, for our 640 acres of land are lying in an unproductive state, and Nancy's money is all in the States, excepting $200, which were sent across the plains.

The spring here opens early this year, a full month in advance of last. The hillsides are covered with good fresh grass and many places with a variety of flowers, some of which would adorn a garden.

The pony that we called "Uncle Ned" is gone "where the good ponies go"—to the mines. I got a mare and $15 for it, but after it had run out a few weeks, and improved, it became so wild that I could not catch it, and I gave a man $2.00 to catch her for me. But I have traded again, and this time I have got one that Nancy can ride, and could be sold for $100.

We have got but one cow at home, and one in the Willammette Valley, and $75 there for the purpose of buying another cow.

Alice is growing fast, and can stand by holding to a chair. Nancy is going to put a lock (a small lock I guess) of her hair in this book. She has two teeth and Nancy says she can bite.

I understand that Jesse Dryer is here, with Rawson. He sent word to me that you had sent a box and that it was in his trunk at Marysville and would be brought to this valley as soon as there was an opportunity. Marysville is a place in the Willammette, about 100 miles from here. The country is beginning to be pretty well settled up in this quarter, some new neighbors having lately come in. Our claim is joined on three sides by settlers.

There is a new post office nearer than Winchester, to which I would like you to direct hereafter. Name, Deer Creek, Douglass County.

I have not received a letter from Sarah yet. I will still look for it. I received a letter from John. I will send an answer in a short time.

April 17. I have just received a letter from Nancy's folks in relation to her property, which we will probably get this fall. I start for the Willammette next Wednesday, and will be gone about 15 days, I shall bring a cow with me, perhaps two. I shall take this book with me and mail it in the Willammette. While I am gone Nancy will have to stay alone, excepting one of the neighbors little girls. Cattle have rose to an enormous price lately, good oxen will sell for $300.00 per yoke.

I intend when I am able to buy a good horse team, and then I can go somewhere in some reasonable time, and with pleasure. Nancy will send some specimens of wild flowers between the leaves of this book.

C. W. SMITH.

FOOTNOTE:

Norman Rawson of Victor, N. Y., uncle of Mrs. Herman Boughton, who now owns the pistol that he carried across the plains. Dryer was also from Victor.—EDITOR.

"Ever changing from scene to scene, deriving new interest from them all, and learning each day something more of the many wonders of nature."—The Author.

In the Spring of 1850 the startling reports from California in relation to the discoveries of gold had been generally confirmed and sustained by such a vast number of letters that most men were satisfied of their truth.

Strongly impressed with the general correctness of reports from the modern El Dorado, I at length determined to wend my way in that direction, and having made the necessary arrangements, I left Centreville, Ind., on the second of April, 1850. On the same day a company of about twelve men left the same place and about the same number left Richmond, Ind., bound for the same destination.

The Spring of 1850 was unusually backward, in consequence of which many were compelled to spend many days at the various starting places on the frontier.

April 4, 1850.

I make my first note at Cincinnati, Ohio, on board the Cambria April 4, 1850. Though the Spring is backward, the weather has been fine for a few days past; some parts have begun to assume a green appearance, and the roads from this place were quite good.

I have engaged passage on the Cambria for St. Louis, and am now impatient to be off. The boat was to start at 4 o'clock P. M., but we are yet here. It is a very common practice of deceiving travelers as to the time of the departure of boats. It should be frowned down by the traveling public, as it causes great perplexity and loss of time, etc. Passengers are still coming on board. Most of them are bound for California. A large number of mules and horses are on deck. Some of them are inferior animals, especially the mules. The price of mules and horses is represented as being quite high at St. Joseph and Independence. Good wagons can be purchased here for $75.00, and many are being taken for the emigrating service. A company has been organized here, offering to carry passengers to the gold region for $160, each passenger to do his equal share of the necessary labor upon the road.

April 5, 1850.

Ohio River, April 5, 1850. We left Cincinnati yesterday afternoon about 5 o'clock, with a large number of passengers on board. Reached Madison last night and laid to till morning. We are now riding along at a fine rate. The clouds that hung above us all the morning are partly cleared away, and the warm sun shining through at intervals, making it rather pleasant and it would be really so, were it not for a cold breeze that is now up. The trees upon the banks of the river begin to assume the appearance of spring, putting forth their fresh buds and lending to the prospect some degree of cheerfulness. The banks of the river are here high and abrupt, and well timbered, though the general prospect is rather monotonous.

Sunday, April 7.

I made no note of yesterday, having seen nothing of particular interest. The river banks become lower as we descend. Today I have seen fruit trees in blossom. Our passage is rather disagreeable—too cool to be agreeable on deck, from which the passenger wishes to view the shores of the river. I rose early this morning and went on deck, as usual. It was early dawn, so early that I would not have thought it morning were it not for a golden streak in the east, glowing beneath a heavy mass of dark clouds. We were just then at an interesting point, passing round the point from the Ohio into the mighty Mississippi, and had already begun to stem its muddy current when I came on deck. I took a long look down between her banks, for the purpose of impressing upon my memory a picture which I might unveil in the future. The flush of crimson dawn-light was reflected upon the ripples that came chasing in our wake.

Now and then upon the shore the dark outlines of a log cabin (the wood-chopper's home) met the eye. The banks are low and marshy, and mostly covered with underbrush, such as cottonwood, etc. The river is some two miles wide here (fifteen miles above the mouth of the Ohio) and divided by numerous islands of all sizes—from an acre to several miles in length. To keep the channel, we have to shift constantly from one side of the river to the other; sometimes I could throw a stone to the shore. This is a quiet, calm Sabbath morning, the sun shining out brightly, with a cool breeze floating in from the west. But the iron giant beneath us knows no Sabbath, no more than those who direct her powerful arms, and keeps working on, tireless and undismayed; but like a war horse, champing the bit, he is a dangerous slave, breathing fire and smoke and shaking his person by his gigantic struggles. To use a strong poetical figure, he seems to say:

"Bind me down with your iron bands, Make sure of your curb and rein, For I scorn the strength of your puny hands As the lion scorns a chain."

The California-bound passengers on board are a hardy-looking class of men, say but little about the gold, and are probably prepared to meet the dangers and hardships of the journey.

April 8.

The banks of the Mississippi begin to assume a more cheerful aspect, the banks are higher and are partly covered with cedar bushes and other evergreen shrubbery. We arrived at St. Louis at about 9 o'clock this morning, and immediately took passage upon "The Pride of the West" for St. Joseph. We expect to be about a week in going there, longer than it would take to travel the same distance on the Ohio, owing to the numerous obstructions in the river. The signs of an immense emigration become more apparent as we approach the starting points. Every boat is crowded with passengers, horses, wagons and everything else necessary for an outfit preparatory to crossing the continent.

At St. Louis business appears quite brisk at present. The levee is crowded with articles of trade. But St. Louis, like Louisville, bears the mark of slavery in their population and the appearance of local business; their suburbs, instead of being occupied by the beautiful little dwellings of artisans, look ruinous and uninteresting.

Well, we are under way again, St. Louis is fading away in the twilight and blending with the distant hills. Tomorrow morning I expect to look upon the waters of the Missouri.

April 9.

We entered the Missouri this morning at sunrise and are now making but slow progress in consequence of the numerous obstructions in the stream, such as sawyers, sand bars, etc. We are compelled to lie up at shore at night. The weather is decidedly cool today, and we have been favored with a few flakes of snow. The soil some sixty miles above St. Louis looks productive, is sufficiently high for agricultural purposes and is well timbered. At St. Louis I saw a few Indians, belonging to some of the western tribes. They were dressed in the highest style of their fashion, their faces painted and highly colored with red powder. Their hair is also dyed or powdered red after the same manner as their faces. They were quite curious specimens of humanity to those unacquainted with Indian fashions. We have but very few lady passengers.

April 10.

Weather clear and cold. We have just passed Jefferson City, the capital of Missouri. It is but a small place and unimportant, only as being the capital. The state house is a respectable two-story stone building situated upon a bluff near the river, fronting the east. There is also a state prison here, inclosed by a high stone wall. We have seen some specimens of wild game on the river, such as geese, ducks, turkeys, etc. Speaking of game reminds me of gaming, a business that is very extensively followed on the river steamers. About one third of the passengers on board are at this moment engaged in that laudable profession—many of them play for money. This class is bound for California and pass the dimes freely.

April 13.

I have neglected my journal a little on account of sickness. The boat is anything but agreeable to a person in good health, but to a sick man it is almost insupportable. When I awoke yesterday morning, I was very much oppressed with heat, and supposed the weather had moderated in the night. I got up and went on deck, and fancied that the weather was very mild, but instead of this, I suppose the difference was in myself, having contracted a slight fever in the night. In cooling myself I caught a severe cold, and soon began to feel very chilly. I sat by a hot stove, wrapped in my overcoat, but it was impossible to get warm, so I sat shivering all day. Owing to the crowded state of the boat, I had not got a berth when I took passage, but slept upon the cabin floor, with about fifty others. I again attempted to get a berth, but could not, so I was compelled to "chew the cud of sweet and bitter fancy" alone. Today I succeeded in getting a berth of one of the passengers, in which I took a refreshing sleep, took some quinine, and now begin to feel better. I also had a very severe pain in my side, but I am getting better of that, too. As I have been close by the stove for a day or two past, I can say but little about the country through which I have passed. Yet I know we have run upon numerous sand bars, backed out and found other channels; stopped for wood and passengers, and I felt the jarring of the machinery beneath me. A large number of the passengers on board are more or less indisposed, so I have not suffered more than many others. We have passed several respectable towns in coming up, the principal of which are Boonville, Lexington and Independence. The latter is some four miles from the river. We expect to reach St. Joseph tomorrow. There is a report abroad that the cholera prevails at St. Joseph, and some of our passengers are leaving the boat to avoid it. It is also said to prevail at other towns on

the river. I shall not deviate from my course on that account. If it is my fate to be stricken down at this time, I shall try to meet my fate like a Christian. But I have hope and a strong belief that—
"There's a divinity that shapes our ends Rough hew them how we will."

April 18.

Weston, Missouri, April 18. We arrived here last Sunday morning, stopped, because our boat being a large one, we could not go up the river in her further. We have since concluded that Weston is as good a starting-place as any on the Missouri, and have determined to fit out here for the journey, and we have already engaged partners in a wagon, looked at cattle, provisions, etc.

April 22.

Our arrangements are completed, and we intend to cross the river tomorrow and join a company as soon as possible. The weather is becoming a little more pleasant, as the Spring is late. We will take with us what grain we can carry for our cattle. I am now enjoying good health and feel myself hardening to our present rude mode of life. All that now remains to be done is to put our cattle to the wagon and be off.

April 23.

Weston Ferry, April 23. As we found several parties before us at the ferry this morning, we are compelled to wait several hours till our turn. All we expect today is to cross the river, and go out two or three miles in the country, where we expect to join a company. Several hundred wagons are already on the opposite shore, waiting for the season to bring forth grass, etc. I can now see the smoke ascending from the camp fires behind the bluff upon the other side. Everybody is impatient to be on the trail, fearing that others will reach the diggings before him. Two of our party are quite feverish just now, and I have consented to start immediately, though I think it is too early.

The ferry boats here are very poor and make slow passages. Common flat boats are used, propelled with oars; they have to tow them up the shore a quarter of a mile before crossing, to prevent landing below their mark on the other side. They carry about two wagons each time, beside several head of cattle or horses. We are now to cross.

April 25.

We started early this morning from our encampment one mile west of the Missouri, and went to within about one mile of a stream called Soldiers' Creek. We have not yet joined a company. Today we made some 18 miles. About noon we stopped at the cabin of an old Indian, of whom we purchased an additional supply of corn at $1.00 per barrel. The country through which we came today is a high, rolling prairie.

April 26.

Left our encampment about 8 o'clock in the morning and went some fifteen miles before stopping, where we encamped for the night. We stopped by a fine little stream of excellent water. Today I had some extensive views entirely different from any I ever before experienced. Everything here seems created on a magnificent plan, the atmosphere clear, the landscape just beginning to wear its earliest green, and the landscape stretched far back against the sky. Today we fell in with some other Californians, but, having mule teams, they soon left us in the rear. I have not yet seen any game except a few prairie hens. I have seen but very few Indians. Today we met one brawny fellow; he was quite sociable—wanted whiskey and "tobac." We gave him a small piece of the latter. He was very thankful for small favors, and as he left us, he took a trail and was soon lost sight of among the hills. He wore buckskin leggings, a blanket over his shoulders, and a sort of turban on his head. Last night I stood on guard till 12 o'clock. Profound silence reigned, except the croaking of a million frogs, and the distant rumbling of thunder in a black cloud that hung in the west. In the latter part of the night it rained a little. The grass is very poor here, but is said to be better several miles in advance.

April 27.

Was off early this morning, and traveled about thirty miles over a fine prairie country. I saw a large train of wagons that came in on the St. Joseph road. I have noticed a great many ox teams on the road. I believe they make the surest team—will subsist on nearly anything and are not so liable to become fractious and run away, if properly managed, as horses or mules. The weather is still cold—it must be extremely cold here in winter.

April 28.

Set off about sunrise and drove about twenty miles and stopped. Owing to our ignorance of the road, we had some trouble to find a convenient place to encamp, the country getting a little more level.

April 29.

This morning we joined a company of three wagons with which we intend to travel. The men are mostly Germans and not of my selection. Went about twenty miles by one o'clock and encamped; high winds prevail. We all have good health and strong appetites. A sort of inefficient election was held this morning at which one of our men was chosen captain—a man in no way calculated to act in that capacity. Strong pledges of mutual assistance were given, etc. In looking over these vast prairies, just beginning to freshen beneath the smile of Spring, I can scarcely believe that they are uninhabited. Not a tree is within reach of the eye.

April 30.

Off again early this morning and went seven miles before breakfast. After breakfast we pushed on twelve miles more by one o'clock, when we stopped to dine, by a small brook. Two miles more brought us to another stream, which we crossed, and traveled on. Yesterday afternoon a mild south wind prevailed, but fell in the night, when it became quite cold. Toward morning, a perfect gale sprung up in the north, and though I laid in the wagon, wrapped in a blanket, in heavy overcoat, I suffered very much by the cold. The wind poured through our covering like cold water. Thirty wagons passed us today—they all had feed for their teams. The wind still raged this morning till about noon, when the sun shone out and it began to get pleasant.

The country here assumes a more even appearance, and resembles in some degree what I had anticipated. We have seen a great number of little animals called prairie squirrels, resembling the ground squirrel of the northern states. The ground is literally filled with their holes. I have seen also a great many elk horns by the way; they are huge specimens and indicate that a superior quality of game abounds here at certain seasons of the year. A few prairie hens come in sight occasionally, but are rather wild. No timber except on the water courses, and upon these it is so hedged in by the hills that it cannot be seen till you get close to it. In consequence of their ignorance of the road, the emigrants carry wood and water where it is unnecessary, and again, neglect to take it when needed; but this is unavoidable. The heavy west winds drive a blinding dust in our faces, and in a few hours a person becomes as black as a negro. Yesterday we met two United States dragoons. They report some Indian depredations in advance of us. One is that a family has been massacred by the Indians, and that the troops from the Fort Laramie had pursued the murderers and put one hundred to death. Our road so far has been most excellent, better than a turnpike, as it is not so hard for the feet of teams. Generally the road is not worn through the heavy turf but just deep enough to expose the roots of the grass, which are as large as a man's little finger. Yet, from the appearance of the road, there are a great many emigrants before us. Five four-horse wagons passed us yesterday; they traveled fast, intended to go forty per day and had feed sufficient for fifteen days, thirty miles.

May 1.

Started early and went to a tributary of Little Blue River, some four miles, and took breakfast. The grass begins to look better. At noon we found water close by the road. We are constantly passing and re-passing wagons. I have noticed some few families on the road, including all ages and sexes. Tonight we stop off the road to the right one hundred rods, within four miles of Big Blue River. We cross it tomorrow. The country tolerably level. The wolves make a great noise at night. A majority of the emigrants now on the road are Missourians. Distance, twenty-four miles.

May 2.

Left encampment at two o'clock this morning, for the purpose of giving our cattle more time to feed in the middle of the day. Reached Blue River at daylight; crossed over immediately; went two miles further and stopped for breakfast. This plan of irregular driving I consider of no advantage, yet we have practiced it because some of our men think it excellent policy. Weather fine, with a shower in the afternoon. Today we passed the place where the Weston road joins the Independence and St. Joseph roads. Many come in from the Independence road, and the trail is now alive with emigrants. At night we stopped twelve miles west of Big Blue River, a short distance from the road, where we found wood, water and some picking for our cattle. When I got up this morning I felt quite unwell and soon commenced vomiting. Mr. Finch offered me his pony to ride, which I accepted, but soon found it almost impossible to keep my seat, so I got off and led the pony. Soon after, one of our company solicited the use of the pony, and as I let him have it and he rode on, I was compelled to walk till we stopped for breakfast. I felt so exhausted that it was almost impossible to proceed, and at one time I seriously thought of lying down by the road and resting myself, and run the risk of losing the wagons. But I struggled on till breakfast time, when I took medicine and soon became better. In many places in this region we find water standing in holes upon the prairie, and as the weather is cool it is tolerably good, though I suppose it stagnates later in the season.

May 3.

Started early; soon crossed a little stream and went on in a northwest direction till noon, when we came round to the southwest. Up to this time our general course has been northwest, and this is the reason why the season seems so backward here. The vegetation is no more advanced here than at Weston ten days since. We were passed at noon by a company of one hundred wagons from Wisconsin, and also one of thirty from Illinois. Most of them had fine horse teams— generally four horses to each wagon. The wind has been high and cold—cold as winter. Imagine a man on the third of May walking in a heavy overcoat and blanket, and shivering with cold. This was my condition. At sundown the wind subsided and a rosy glow in the west promised a fair tomorrow. Went nineteen miles today and stopped by a little stream called Rock Brook. I see but very few Indians, perhaps one in a week. We have passed the Potawatimes region, and are now in that of the Pawnees. I have seen none of the latter tribe. Today we met a few troops from Fort Laramie. They say the grass is good in the valley of the Platte, distant about one hundred miles. Good health on the road generally, though we see a grave occasionally, which reminds us of the admonition, "memento mori," and beneath this inhospitable soil are hearts once virtuous ambition. The angel of death follows the race of Adam to the uttermost parts of the earth.

"There is no flock however watched and tended, But one dead lamb is there; There is no fireside howso'er defended, But has one vacant chair."

May 4.

Today we made some eighteen miles—passed two or three little streams, and encamped about one mile from the road, by a stream of good water. Weather pleasant and warm in the afternoon. Met one team returning on account of poor grass in advance. It is tolerable where we stop tonight in a valley.

May 5.

Today we rested, partly to observe the Sabbath and partly to let our teams rest. The day has been fair, with a cool breeze from the north. Sun sets gloriously, with fair promise of tomorrow. About fifty wagons went by us today, while others are stopping near us. Our men are now engaged in the business of the closing day—feeding cattle, etc., and others loitering about the wagon and thinking, perhaps, of Sabbath evenings spent in a different manner.

May 6.

Off at sunrise. Reached Little Blue River in the evening. Day fine. We crossed several valleys in which were channels filled with yellow sand. It is probable that water courses through them during the wet seasons. Grass poor. Emigrants pushing by us. The Little Blue River is a fine stream about ten yards in width and deep.

May 7.

Went up by Little Blue River fifteen miles, and encamped about 4 o'clock, earlier than usual, for the purpose of repairing wagon wheels. We are getting into the buffalo region; one was seen yesterday and one killed today by a man in another company. I have seen none yet. Prairie hens are abundant, and I have had the pleasure of partaking of one myself. Day fine, excepting a cool breeze.

May 8.

Encamped again by Little Blue River, after a drive of fifteen miles. This morning we met a young man in search of a pony, which had strayed away from him in the night. He looked quite discouraged, and well he might, as the lost nag was his only means of conveying his provisions and clothes. They suspected the Indians. Presently we came up to his comrades, where we found their things in great confusion, and the man with them in a gloomy mood. But they were partially relieved by some gentlemen who were there when we came up, who offered to buy their things or carry them for them, as they might prefer. It looks hard to meet misfortunes so soon, but many have had to submit to them, as is apparent all along the route. Horses, mules and oxen have died, wagons have broken down, and sickness fell to the lot of some. Some of the teams have consumed all of their feed and begin to travel more moderately. In this case they are compelled to go slow, as the grass is very poor. Roads today good and scenery pleasant.

May 9.

Commenced our march at sunrise, and drove our cattle slowly on account of the poor feed they had had. Went up the Little Blue twelve miles, when we left it and entered a high prairie country. Distance, sixteen miles.

May 10.

Went on as usual. Met some government wagons going to Fort Leavenworth. Drove eighteen miles and encamped at the border of the Platte River bottom. The river itself is some four miles distant, and there is no water nearer, nor wood, so we are compelled to do without it and make our supper of hard bread, etc. But little promise of grass. Day pleasant.

May 11.

Went four miles to the Platte before breakfast. Just opposite where we stopped is a large island and but a narrow stream on this side; the water is very muddy. We reached Fort Kearney about 4 o'clock, ten miles further, and stopped for the night one mile west of the fort. At Fort Kearney there are several plain-looking buildings, mostly composed of unburnt brick and turf, and some tents, though the best houses are wood. One hundred fifty soldiers are stationed here. We hope to reach Fort Laramie by the end of the month. Grass looks a little better in the valley. Day warm. Distance, fifteen miles.

May 12.

This day being Sunday, we rest ourselves, and cattle are in need of it. About one hundred wagons have passed us today; at times the road would be crowded with them for a great distance.

May 13.

Having rested yesterday, we made an early start this morning, and went five miles before stopping to take breakfast. Then went twelve miles farther and encamped for the night near the river. The stream at this point is from one to two miles wide, shallow, and divided by numerous islands. Though there is plenty of timber up on the opposite shore, and the islands, we have not yet been able to get a stick upon this side—not enough for fuel. All day we have seen wagons winding along on the opposite shore, on the road from Council Bluffs. The valley of the river here is broad and beautiful, stretches away as far as the eye can reach, and occasionally presenting upon its blue and white profile herds of buffalo, deer, elk, antelope, etc. Distance, seventeen miles.

May 14.

Some of our cattle having strayed off, we were delayed a short time in finding them. However, we were under way at seven o'clock. Having encamped last night with three additional wagons, we all started together this morning, and I hope we may continue so. Our new associates appear like upright men—men who would respect justice where there is no law. At night we stopped one mile west of Plum Creek in a most delightful place, the beauty of which I am incapable of faithfully delineating. Distance, seventeen miles.

May 15.

Off early, pursuing our course up the Platte; valley wide and bordered by high bluffs; at places they are divided by deep ravines, giving us a peep at the background. Today one of our party had the good luck to kill an antelope, and we had the pleasure of partaking of it for supper. The meat is very sweet and tender, and after living for nearly a month on salt pork, it was decidedly relishable. The Indians visit the road but very little, which is not much regretted by the emigrants. Last night a man came to one of our wagons who was in search of horses, which had become frightened and ran away from his company. They lost nine, which were all they had. This is a great loss. The grass is but little better here than it was at Weston; the season has been cold and dry. Distance, twenty-two miles.

May 16.

Traveled over a level country; saw some antelope and was passed by a train of wagons from Galena, Wis. Tonight we stopped near the river. I never saw finer horses than are on this road, especially those from Wisconsin and Illinois. Distance, fifteen miles.

May 17.

Continued our march over beautiful prairie country, and encamped in the afternoon upon a green plain not far from the Platte. I forgot to mention before that when we reached the fort but nine hundred wagons had been reported as having passing this Spring, and about one hundred more have gone ahead since then. From this we perceive that we are comparatively among the first of the emigrants this season. A few pass us every day, but as we are passing others, it is difficult to tell how many really keep in advance of us. Distance, fifteen miles.

May 18.

In our course today we left the Platte several miles to the right and entered on a high region. At noon we stopped by a small stream of good water, which winds along in an easterly direction between the hills and the river. In the evening we stopped on the same stream higher up. Grass poor. Today we met a man who was in search of a horse which had run away from him in a buffalo herd. He had himself become lost, a considerable distance from the road, was without food or arms, except a single pistol. Saw numerous herds of buffalo and represented the country as barren and desolate. His horse had been taken up by another company, and when we saw him, he was in search of his own. Day warm. Distance, seventeen miles.

May 19.

In consequence of there being little grass where we stopped last night, we were off early this morning, and intended to cross the south fork of the Platte before we stopped, which we supposed was about ten miles distant. Today I saw almost countless numbers of buffalo. I saw several shot and a great many dead by the road. They are huge animals, some of them larger than any I ever saw; ran in a clumsy sort of canter, yet they are not slow, as it takes a good horse to overtake them. A man stayed with us last night who had got lost while in pursuit of the game. He and another man had killed three, and had some choice cuts with them. In the morning I lent my rifle to one of our party who wished to go hunting. In a couple of hours he came up with the gun broken; he said it was done in a hand-to-hand encounter with a buffalo. But I shall not state the particulars, as I have reason to discredit his story. About noon we reached the south fork of the Platte and crossed it immediately. This river where we cross it is about one mile wide, with an average depth of about one foot. It is entirely different from any other river I ever saw in the States. The bed of the river is a kind of quicksand, into which a horse will sink several inches by standing still a few moments. Another of our men has just returned from buffalo hunting. He succeeded in killing one, but not till he had fired twelve bullets at it. The balls at the head rebounded as from the solid rock. This evening one of our men found a human skull near our wagons. It was perforated by a ball just above the left eye and through the back of the head. We examined it and conjectured how it came here—whether Indian or white, male or female. But all our conjectures could not draw from its eyeless hole one ray of its history, nor awake a slumbering echo in its hollow ear. "Alas, poor Yorick! Is that a place where a god may dwell?" We have passed more than fifty wagons today. In the afternoon a thunder shower came up in the west, and for two or three hours threatened heavy rain; and at length, after shedding a few drops, it passed round to the south. We have been just one week in coming from Fort Kearney, a distance of 125 miles. At this rate we shall reach Fort Laramie by the first of June. The grass is poor in this region, and is never so good here as in the districts we have passed. I have not seen an Indian in two weeks, but I presume they have seen us every day. Distance, fifteen miles.

May 20.

We continued our march up the south fork of the Platte some ten miles, where we crossed over the bluffs which lie between the two streams, and after going two miles we reached the north fork at about noon. In the afternoon we continued up on the south side of the north flat. At this point the river wears the same general characteristics as the lower Platte. The banks are lower and the soil less productive, but the stream is wide, shallow, and filled with islands or sand-bars. Tonight we feed our cattle on two of these little islands, near the south shore. The grass is very poor here. Two of our party who went out yesterday morning to hunt have not yet returned. It is very easy to get lost on these vast wilds, as the country is very much alike, and in pursuing game, the uninitiated thinks of very little beside. Distance, twenty miles.

May 21.

This morning, after going some two miles up the banks of the river, we turned off to the south and wound up over the bluffs, and traveled a level, dry region, almost destitute of vegetation. After going over this tableland for about twelve miles, we again came down to the river, through a steep and sandy ravine. Our feet would sink into the sand some six or eight inches in walking over it, and was thrown up in showers by the wheels of our wagons. We stopped for the night some twelve miles farther beyond where we reached the bottom. The day has been warm, though cloudy. The earth is parched with drought, and if rain does not fall soon, vegetation will be entirely checked. The flood of emigrants is rushing past and behind us, all in haste to surpass each other in reaching the land of gold. Some of the fastest travelers have already gained much time upon us; a few have gone by us who started as late as the fifth and sixth of May. But they are now compelled to go more slow, as the feed with which they supplied themselves on the start is exhausted, and their teams are becoming weak. One of our party waded across the Platte today for the purpose of ascertaining the condition of the grass on the other side, as from our side it looks quite forward. The water was nowhere above his knees. Two of our men who left us on Sunday for the purpose of hunting buffaloes have returned. They were completely tired of their sport, having succeeded in capturing one of those huge animals and wounding half a dozen more. Distance, nineteen miles.

May 22.

After going up the Platte two miles from camp, we left the stream and went over the bluffs, in consequence of the river banks being high and broken. The road was not so good today, as we had to go through deep sand most of the way. We stopped at night at the mouth of Ash Hollow, at which place the road that goes up the South Platte came in. At the lower end there are several springs and a little timber, such as ash and cedar, and some shrubbery. We are now in the territory of the Sioux Indians, a party of whom are now about our wagons. They are very desirous to beg or buy provisions, particularly sugar, coffee, and liquor. The chief was here and made himself known to us. Their dress is very simple and confined to adults, the children going naked, except a bit of cloth fastened about their loins. This tribe is quite friendly, and the chief signified that anything that we might lay out of our wagons would be perfectly safe. They look quite intelligent for Indians and superior to what I had expected to see. Some of them are now practicing with their bows and arrows for the amusement of the emigrants. The wind has been very high all day and the dust troublesome. The sun has just sunk down in the west, casting a crimson flush upon the dark clouds that hang like a dark curtain drawn across the west. Companies of emigrants have encamped all around us, and should the Indians make an attack upon us, at least two hundred men could be gathered in ten minutes. Distance, twenty-five miles.

May 23.

Today we continued our travel over a sandy soil, making slow progress in consequence. We set out at daybreak, and after going a couple of miles, came to an Indian village. They live in tents made of buffalo skins. These skins they support on poles set round in a circle on the ground, and fastened together at the top. In cold weather they make their fires in the center of the tent and have an aperture in the top for the smoke to escape. These Indians, like all others, are always ready to trade, and will sometimes give enormous prices for articles they happen to fancy. Sugar and coffee are prized very highly by them. I have known them to give from $1 to $3 per pint for the first, and as they seem to have plenty of money just now, it will be a profitable trade for those who have a surplus of these articles. Before I left the United States I was not aware that these articles could be sold at such prices among the Indians. Distance, twenty miles.

May 24.

Traveling two miles this morning, we came to another Indian encampment of some thirty-five tents. They were encamped upon a beautiful and expansive plain. These Indians are of the same character of those we saw yesterday. When we passed by, the sun was just rising and the scene was quite picturesque. These Indians have a large number of ponies and mules, which were scattered over the valley feeding, while several Indians in their blue and white blankets and buffalo skins were watching them. There were four or five dogs about each tent, and as we passed they gave us a satisfactory display of vocal sounds. These dogs are an inferior-looking brute and from imagination appear a little wolfish. They howl rather than bark, and when a number of them are in concert, it sounds singularly mournful and plaintive. The road becomes better as we advance and the grass better than we have before seen. In fact, this is the earliest period at which the grass can be considered fit for working cattle. Distance, twenty miles.

May 25.

A short distance beyond our stopping place we crossed a small stream called Small Creek. Soon after, we came in sight of those promised curiosities, the Courthouse and Chimney Rock, the first appearing in the distance like the dome of an immense building and the latter like a tower or straight column. At noon, we came nearly opposite the Court House, and as it appeared but a short distance from the road, some of our men determined to go to it and satisfy their curiosity. They went, and by fast walking, overtook us about four o'clock in the afternoon. It is about seven miles from the trail, and appears very fine, being discernable from all points. It is composed of an immense mass of rock, raising from 300 to 500 feet above the level of the plain, and of a conical shape at the summit, from which it derives its name. Chimney Rock is about twelve miles further, and seven miles from where we stop tonight. At noon we crossed another stream, the largest since we crossed Little Blue River, and good water. It comes in from the south, a little east of the Court House. This afternoon we had a fine specimen of a hail storm in this region. A dark mass of clouds were gathering for several hours in the west, till our path was overhung with an impenetrable curtain of black, and at length the wind, which was blowing from the east, turned back, and the storm rushed upon us. It was a real hail storm. When it commenced beating upon our cattle, they became intractable, but we succeeded in unfastening them from the wagons, and having driven them behind the wagons, they bore it as well as might have been expected. The hail stones were the largest I ever saw, some of them being as large as hens' eggs, and striking with force sufficient to make a man seek a shelter as soon as convenient. It continued some twenty minutes, when it stopped and we commenced our march; but we had not gone far when it recommenced, and we were compelled to turn around and wait till it ceased. But we have reason to be thankful, as we did not feel the worst of the storm. Two of our men who were in advance to find a stopping-place for the night were less fortunate than ourselves. Where they were, the hailstones were as large as lemons and with force enough to bruise a man severely. Our party in advance were on horses, and as they became fractious, they could not shelter themselves, and had to take the full force of the storm. One of our men received a severe bruise on his head, caused by a hailstone. But the storm soon blew over and the sun set behind a crimson curtain of transparent clouds. Distance, twenty miles.

May 26.

Today being Sunday, we determined to lay by till noon and let our cattle rest, and go on in the afternoon to the vicinity of Chimney Rock, which would afford better feed and give us an opportunity to examine this great natural curiosity. A large number of teams passed us in the forenoon, which made some of our party impatient to be going. I said we stopped to let our cattle rest, for the men were nearly all engaged in such matters as become necessary, such as washing their clothes, airing their bedding, and such other things as could not be done on the way. By four o'clock we were opposite Chimney Rock, and after going a short distance further we stopped for the night. In company with some others of our party, I started for the Rock, some two miles distant. The lower portion of it is thrown up like a mound in a conical shape, to the height of about two hundred feet, and upon this rests a perpendicular column of some twenty feet in diameter, and about one hundred feet high. By some, the height of the rock is computed at from five hundred to eight hundred feet, but I have put it as it appeared to me. The lower portion is composed of baked clay, and the upper part of a kind of soft rock, darker in color than the base. I saw thousands of names which were engraved upon the plaster material, and intended to carve my own, but was prevented by a storm coming on. It continued to rain that evening, and as there was a cold wind, and we had no fuel except a little we had in our wagons, it was anything but pleasant; but as we went to bed early, we soon forgot the rain beneath comfortable blankets. Though the ground was wet, a good buffalo robe was sufficient to keep out dampness all night. High bluffs are visible on each side of us, and in advance. Distance, eight miles.

May 27.

For a few days past we have got up and started about two o'clock in the morning, and so we did this morning. So after we set out, it recommenced raining and continued till we stopped for breakfast. Some of our men swore if they were at home they would not be caught here again, and it was disagreeable, trying to kindle a fire of wet fuel, being wet ourselves, and still getting more damp and chilly if possible. But at length the clouds broke away, and having refreshed ourselves with some warm breakfast, we went on our way rejoicing. We left the river in the early part of the day, and traveled upon a high plain, with Scotts Bluffs as the boundary. In the evening we reached the bluffs, where we encamped. In this region wood and water is very scarce, and we were not able to collect during the day so much as we needed; but this might be remedied by taking them in previously if we had known what was in advance. At the Bluffs we found several little springs, but they were between such precipitous banks that it was almost impossible to get our cattle to them, and some of them entirely beyond their reach. Here we found a little wood, consisting of a few specimens of stunted cedar scattered upon the bluffs and in the ravines, and a little dry wood in the valley, having been washed down by the rain. This latter is most excellent fuel, having been exposed to the sun for years, and as dry as powder. Some of the best teams begin to go our pace and will be thankful if they can maintain it. Distance, twenty-three miles.

May 28.

After proceeding a couple of miles, we came to an Indian encampment and also a place where blacksmithing was done, and on a little further we ascended the bluffs and traveled over a level, high country and came to the Platte again in the afternoon and encamped at night in the valley of that stream. This morning we had the first view of the Rocky Mountains, 150 miles distant. Laramie Peak looks like a vast sugar loaf. We see a little timber today by the Platte, such as cedar, pine and poplar. Day warm, and sand deep. Distance, twenty-five miles.

May 29.

After traveling five miles, we came to a trading place, which was occupied by some half dozen men and some thirty or forty Sioux Indians. They had clothing, but no provisions, which were most sought by the emigrants. This place is within twenty miles of Fort Laramie, and we have been so successful in getting over the ground that we feel no small degree of gratification. At three o'clock we came to Laramie River and forded it and encamped about one half mile beyond by the road opposite the Fort, which is a mile or more to the south of it. In consequence of the lateness of our arrival and the determination of our party to proceed early in the morning, I could not find time to visit it, but was compelled to satisfy my curiosity at a distance. From where I now am I can see several respectable looking buildings, looking the most like civilization of anything that I have seen since I left Weston. Laramie River has the same characteristics as the Platte, only much smaller, and about four feet deep where we forded it. A large number of emigrants change their mode of travel at this place—from wagons to packing—for the purpose of hastening their arrival in the gold regions. In doing this, some of them abandon much property, such as guns, tools, bedding, clothing, and more especially wagons and harness. I was told last evening that two men had just thrown their rifles into the Platte, having tried to sell them to no purpose, and being determined that no one should profit by the loss. Good wagons can be bought for a mere trifle, and many of them can be had for nothing. An excellent one was sold here yesterday at $7 and with it a lot of other valuables thrown into the bargain. Near us in this valley there is a very large number of emigrants encamped, stopping for the purpose of some business and seeing the Fort. I should think there were about 500 wagons and 2,000 men. Provisions, biscuit and bacon can be obtained at the Fort in small quantities by those who are in need of them, sufficient to last them to Salt Lake. Biscuit, $14 per pound. Though we are on the first part of our journey, we see many things left by the way, but everything of any value is examined and perhaps taken a short distance by those who come after, when they in turn cast them away; and others still encumber themselves as before. I have seen men take hold of a log chain and drag it for several rods, knowing at the same time that they could not take it with them; but having large acquisitiveness, they would cling to it from the force of habit, or in hopes that some lucky circumstance would turn up that would enable them to sell it. A man was at our camp this morning who had a rifle, a hatchet, and a shovel, which he offered to sell for two dollars, but could not, so he gave the rifle to one of our party and took the rest along. The soil is poor and sandy here and the grass short and dry. Distance, twenty-five miles.

May 30.

At three o'clock this morning we were under way and continued up the Platte, and having gone sixteen miles by two o'clock, we stopped for the night, our cattle being much in need of feed and rest, having traveled hard and found but little feed in the vicinity of the Fort. Some three miles before we stopped we left the river and ascended the tableland, passing over innumerable little knobs, upon which is scattered a little cedar and pine. In a ravine near the camp is an excellent spring of water and tolerably good grass. In the afternoon a dark cloud arose in the west, and soon came thunder and lightning and rain; and now while I am writing it is dancing upon our tent in a fine manner—a manner peculiar to this country. At length the clouds cleared away and our party concluded to proceed a few miles further. Accordingly, we collected our cattle, yoked them, and drove about five miles further. In the afternoon we passed some soldiers who were engaged in burning lime for the Fort. One of them wanted to buy liquor; said he had that day offered $16 per gallon for brandy to an emigrant but could not get it. One of our company sold him a drink of whiskey for fifty cents. Distance, twenty-one miles.

May 31.

Going two miles this morning, we came to a little stream called the Little Cottonweed. Our trail led over a hilly country, presenting every variety of scenery, from the level plain to the bold bluffs, with here a few shrubs of pine and cedar. These evergreens are the only objects generally which enliven the plains in which they are found, as they usually grow in the moist barrens and indescribable places, deep ravines and nearly naked rocks. At length we have come into the region of wild sage so well known and so much hated by the emigrant, as it grows in the most inhospitable regions. It is a low, bushy shrub, with thick and light-colored leaves, resembling to some extent the leaf of the cultivated sage and exhaling a similar scent. Our road is very circuitous. We have, in a few hours, traveled toward every point of the compass. Laramie Peak, which we first saw from Scotts Bluffs, is still in sight, several miles to the south of us. Its snow-capped summit presents a strong contrast to the green hill and prairie, which are just putting on their summer apparel. Today we swapped our wagon for one we found abandoned by the road. We made a good trade. Distance, twenty-one miles.

June 1.

Still among the hills. In the afternoon over a high, level plain. Stopped at night by a little stream, a short distance from the Blue Mountain. Day fine. Distance, twenty-five miles.

June 2.

Today we moved on till we came to a little stream about four miles from our last night's stopping-place. One mile from where we stopped, we crossed a little stream called Mountain Blue. We have not found a more beautiful place than where we stopped today—plenty of wood, water and grass. Day fine; health good. There is a novel feature in this region in the existence of a red sand which gives to the prospect a very picturesque character. I suppose it was caused by volcanic fires, which burned perhaps centuries ago. A soft quality of marble also abounds here, and many of our party have smoothed pieces of it and written or carved their names, dates, and other laconic bits of news upon them for their friends behind them. I cut a level surface upon a piece and wrote thus: "C. W. Smith, Centreville, Indiana. 'On the night's Plutonian shore.' June 2, 1850." The country over which we are passing is becoming very rocky and broken, and I am surprised that we can pass over it with so little difficulty. Sometimes we pass along an extensive range of hills, sometimes through a deep gorge or dry-bed of a stream, and then again winding along a serpentine track, thus ever changing from scene to scene, deriving new interest from them all and learning each day something more of the many wonders of nature. Distance, four miles.

June 3.

Having refreshed ourselves yesterday (Sunday) by the river La Bronte, we proceeded this morning in good spirits; about ten o'clock we crossed the river "a la Psete (Prele?)" ten or twelve feet in width, and at night encamped on La Boisce. Great variety of scenery. At noon we had a heavy shower of rain, which increased the water in the creeks to an almost impassable height. Tonight the sky is obscured by heavy masses of dark clouds that sit with portentous aspect upon the brows of the mountains. The valleys of the tributaries of the Platte through which we have passed are narrow and winding, with little timber, such as willows, lind, cottonwood and poplars, beside a little cedar and pine, in the ravines and on the bluffs. Distance, twenty-three miles.

June 4.

Going nine miles brought us to a stream called Deer Creek, about twenty yards wide and with a strong current. Crossed one more stream during the day. Muddy, crooked creek, and encamped in the valley of the Platte, twelve miles from the stream. Country more level by the Platte. Weather pleasant. Distance, eighteen miles.

June 5.

Distances are very deceptive here. A range of mountains to our left appeared about two miles off; became the object of curiosity to some of our party from the fact that there was snow upon its summit, and so they concluded to walk across the plain and ascend them and get some of the snow, if such it was, which some of them doubted. They started about 2 P. M. and as we laid by this afternoon, they supposed it a good opportunity. At sundown our explorers returned, much fatigued. They had walked the entire afternoon after they had left us. The top of the mountains was about twelve miles distant, and they had been there. They brought a snowball and declared that what they saw was worth their labor. Distance, twelve miles.

June 6.

We started early this morning, in order to get ferried across the Platte before those who stopped behind us over night. One mile's travel brought us to the ferry, and our wagons were taken across without delay. There are three boats running across abreast, though conducted by different men. Price per wagon $4.00. They were not willing to ferry our cattle over, so we drove them up a short distance, and made them swim the stream. The boats are run on a very simple principal and a very good one. A long line is stretched across the river, secured at each end. To this are placed two pulley wheels, which are fastened to ropes attached to the boat at each end, and the forward rope being the shortest, the side of the boat is brought to the force of the current and forced across. Two wagons are placed in a boat each trip, which is made in about ten minutes. All being safely over, about 8 o'clock we resumed our march, leaving the river and following the trail over a high range of country, destitute of wood and water. At noon we stopped a short time at Alkali Pond—very poor water and grass; and being none better within fifteen miles, we pushed on in order to reach them by night. At sundown we came from a stream which comes from what are called Willow Springs, about two miles further on. Stopped here. This being a general stopping place, the grass is poor. The stream is small and the valley narrow. On the upland there is no vegetation worth mentioning, except wild sage, which grows in stunted clumps all over the country. We see mountain peaks to the left and in advance, the first being a range of the Black Hills and the second the Rattlesnake Mountains, I suppose. Distance, twenty-six miles.

June 7.

After traveling over a rough country till noon, we came to Grease Creek and encamped on it near Rattlesnake Rock. We stopped about two o'clock for the purpose of resting and letting our cattle feed, as we had just come over a portion of the route nearly destitute of grass and water. We came by one little stream which is known to be poisonous, the water being strongly impregnated with alkali. We learn by some emigrants since we passed this stream that a company who were ignorant of the nature of the water let their horses drink it, and many of them died in consequence. Distance, fourteen miles.

June 8.

Today at noon we reached the Sweetwater, much elated, as we had been on the muddy Platte for more than twenty days. The river is here about six rods wide, and deep; water tolerably good, not quite clear. Another mile brought us to the far-famed Independence Rock. I climbed up its abrupt, rocky sides, and spent a few minutes in walking about its summit, though I had not time to examine it as I wished. It is composed of solid rock of a light red clay color, about one eighth of a mile long and two hundred feet high. There are huge masses of grotesque rocks lying upon its sides and summit, some of which weighed hundreds of tons and appear as if they could be shoved off by the hand. On the prominent points of this rock are carved and painted thousands of names, in all styles and sizes; some are put high up on the ledges, where it must have been difficult to place them, and others nearer the ground. I looked for a familiar name, but could find none, though I saw all the states inscribed, as the former residences of these pilgrims. One half mile further on we crossed the Sweet Water, and in the afternoon went by what is called The Devil's Gate, a narrow channel of the stream, through a pass of the Rattlesnake Mountains. Looking down into the stream from the rocks hundreds of feet high, it is said that the Sweet Water appears as a mere rivulet. Some of our party climbed to the top of the Gate and boasted of having done some daring climbing. We are now surrounded by mountains, entirely barren, except a few stunted cedars or other evergreens. The range on the south is partly covered with snow. Distance, twenty-two miles.

June 9.

Started in the morning. A shower at noon. Distance, fourteen miles.

June 10.

After proceeding up the river for fourteen miles, we left it for sixteen miles. At night we stopped at the Ice Springs. The water is very bad here, so much so that we dare not let our cattle drink it. We see many evidences of its fatality in the many horses and cattle in the vicinity. Distance, twenty miles.

June 11.

Started early and reached the Sweet Water again about 10 o'clock, having gone some ten miles. We were delayed an hour in the morning to find our cattle that had strayed off. Many of our cattle show the effects of bad water and today our best yoke gave out, having to take them from the wagon and drive them slowly behind. Distance, ten miles.

June 12.

Still by the Sweet Water. The valley is becoming more narrow and the stream more rapid. In advance and a little to the north of our trail, we can see the Wind River Mountains. Their lofty summits are covered with snow, and in their dazzling whiteness appear truly sublime. From their great height and the transparency of the air, they look not far off, though they are probably not less than seventy-five miles. In the afternoon I walked over a body of snow lying near the road, and as it had retreated down the bank, it was interesting to notice how the grass and flowers had followed, a barren space of not more than three yards intervening winter's snow and summer's flowers. Pleasant day, just cool enough to be agreeable. The grass is becoming better, as there are numerous springs in this vicinity, by which it grows. Distance, nineteen miles.

June 13.

Started early this morning and went two and three quarters miles to the North Sweet Water, where we took breakfast and stopped till noon. In the afternoon we crossed Willow Creek, and at night encamped on a fine little brook of crystal water about one mile from the main road. Today we have felt that we are in a high region. We see snow in all directions—on the mountains, on the hills and in the ravines—and here, a few yards above me, an extensive bed reflects the rays of the setting sun over a bed of sweet pink flowers which peep up through the fresh grass. The grass is good here, though rather short. We are now within about ten miles of the South Pass, which we will probably reach by tomorrow noon. We see no longer any of the large companies which overtook us on the outset of the journey. They have invariably broken up into small companies of five or six wagons. This is the best plan, especially when there is no danger to be apprehended from the Indians. It is impossible for large companies to improve the time like small companies. The great difficulty is there is too much hesitation on the plains, which invariably results in disagreement. Distance, eleven miles.

June 14.

After going a little over a mile, we crossed the Sweet Water for the last time, leaving it to our right. At noon we were at the South Pass, where we stopped for a short time. In the afternoon we passed the Pacific Springs and encamped within about two miles of Little Sandy. In the afternoon it rained very hard, and now, at sundown, as heavy a cloud as I ever saw is coming up in the west. Distance, seventeen miles.

June 15.

Quite cool last night, so much so that we could not keep warm between a buffalo robe and two good blankets. The night before last was cold also. Water froze over near our camp. After three miles' travel this morning we came to what is called Dry Sandy. In the valley there is no water at this season of the year. We passed down the valley six miles, when we came to the fork in the roads—the Salt Lake and Subletts (?)—cut off, the former leading down by Sandy and the latter keeping to the right, west. Five miles more brought us to the Little Sandy, where we stopped for the night. Tomorrow we shall go but six miles to Big Sandy, where we shall prepare to cross a desert, as it is called, stretching from that stream to Green River, a distance of forty miles, which is generally traveled in the night. Distance, six miles.

June 16.

Today we laid by to prepare to cross the desert from Big Sandy to Green River. This afternoon I went up this stream about three miles to cut grass for our cattle while crossing the desert. I was engaged half a day in cutting two small sacks full with a knife. Then I came back to the wagons and started down the stream for more grass, but found it more scarce than ever. There is but little grass in this region, excepting the creek bottoms, and they are few and narrow.

June 17.

As it was agreed to start early, I went in company with some others to fetch our cattle from some three miles up the river, where they had been feeding. A snowstorm came on about daybreak and I had the full benefit of it. I walked several miles in search of a couple of ponies that belonged to the company and was at last compelled to return without them. The face of the country there is nearly destitute of vegetation, wild sage, greasewood and an occasional bunch of grass being the entire product of the soil. We left Big Sandy at about eleven and a half A. M. with the intention of traveling all night and reaching Green River the next morning. We pushed on as fast as we could against a strong wind and a blinding dust. A little before sundown we stopped an hour for supper and to feed our cattle, having gone fifteen miles. This over, we entered the night, and the most tedious part of our journey. With the sun went down the wind and we hoped that an agreeable night would follow such a boisterous day. But we were disappointed. A dark cloud overcast the sky and soon a snowstorm came drifting in our faces, and continued all night. At twelve o'clock we stopped to rest and feed our cattle, and then pushed on till eight o'clock in the morning, when we reached the Green River. The country between these streams is not so barren as I was led to suppose. It is but little more so than much of the ground we had passed over before, west of Fort Laramie. Green River is about 1,000 feet lower than Big Sandy. Upon this stretch of forty miles there is not a drop of water, and this is the reason why it is so barren. Our cattle stood the drive very well. In the morning the sun shone out clear and warm and the thin mantle of snow soon disappeared beneath his beams. Distance, forty-six miles.

June 18.

About 7 o'clock this morning we came within sight of Green River, apparently not far off, but several hundred feet below us. After the most disagreeable night's travel I ever experienced, we were elated at the prospect of being so near a stopping-place, but on following the trail we had to go about three miles further before we got down to the river. Green River is about twenty rods wide here and so deep that it has to be ferried. In the Spring it is said it can be forded, but it is swollen now in consequence of the snow melting at its sources. There are two ferries, which charge $7 per wagon. We made arrangements to have ours crossed this evening, and accordingly they were taken over without accident. I am told that four men were drowned the other day in attempting to cross on a raft. Some companies find it difficult to make their horses and cattle swim the stream, but ours went over without trouble. We found the grass rather scarce near the ferry, and drove our cattle three miles up the river, where it was first-rate. In company with three others of our party, I went up about sundown to watch the cattle over night. Nowhere upon the way have I found a more beautiful place than this. The valley of the river is broad and Spring's first fresh carpet of grass adorned with fragrant flowers. The numerous varieties of shrubs divided and subdivided the valley into picturesque lawns, and gave more variety to the scenery. We built a good fire of dry wood, and spreading our buffalo robes upon the grass, we laid down to rest, one watching at a time and being relieved at intervals by the others.

June 19.

This morning we drove the cattle back to the wagons and taking breakfast while our company were preparing to start, we were on the march by 7 o'clock. Here we entered a decidedly mountainous country and our road is very crooked. After winding over and around the mountains for about eight miles, we came to a tributary of Green River, which we expect to travel up for several miles. We went two miles up this stream and rested for an hour or two. We found good grass by driving our cattle across the stream, which is narrow and deep. Quite a ludicrous incident occurred here. As I said, the stream is deep, though narrow, our cattle being compelled to swim it when only eight or ten yards wide. Well, when we were ready to start, somebody must cross over to bring the cattle back. After some equivocations, two men were chosen, and having undressed and went a little higher up the stream, they plunged in, but instead of swimming, they struck their knees upon the bottom, and having raised upright in two feet depth of water, walked the remainder of the way across, amid the laughter of the whole company. We crossed to the south side of the stream about two miles further on and left it. After going seven miles further we came to another, and two miles more, another still, by which we stopped for the night. We see snow all round us and have very cool nights. Distance, nineteen miles.

June 20.

Continued our march over a mountainous country, the most rough I ever saw. From some of the elevations we could see the trail for miles, dotted with men, horses and, more distinctly, the white-covered wagons. We passed numerous small streams, flowing from the mountains. After going about seventeen miles, we reached Ham's Fork of Green River, and encamped four miles beyond it on the open prairie, where we found good grass, and water we had in store. The day has been pleasant, more so than any we have had since we left the Sweet Water. This morning I had a fine view of the Bear River Mountains, about seventy-five miles distance, stretching around the sky from the south to the southwest. Their summits are covered with spotless snow. At Ham's Fork I saw another party of the Snake River Indians. Most of them looked very squalid and miserable, and beg provisions of all they can. They are less prepossessing than the Sioux, though they are well supplied with guns and horses. They are good horsemen and use their sharp-pointed arrows with the certainty of a bullet. The mosquitoes began to trouble us today for the first time. We expect they will lay a long siege to our blood. Distance, twenty-one miles.

June 21.

Country continues very mountainous. In the afternoon we passed over a very high range, to descend which ropes had been used by former emigrants on a trail near the one we took. We had two wheels of our wagon locked for more than a mile, and then it was hard to keep it from running over the cattle. The mosquitoes stick to us like genuine friends, especially during the day; at night it is too cool for them. At noon we stopped by a fine stream of water, in a deep gorge of the mountains. In the afternoon we ascended another high range of mountains, from the summits of which we could see far below us into Bear River Valley. This stream is as large as the Sweet Water, and courses its way through a rich and beautiful valley, from three to six miles in width. We encamped in the valley at night by a large pond of very poor water, but the grass was excellent. Distance, twenty-two miles.

June 22.

Continued down the valley of Bear River. In the forenoon we passed four branches of the stream, which came within a few yards of each other. Some of them were deep and all difficult to cross, but we got over in safety. There is good grass in this valley. Four miles after dinner brought us to Smith's Fork, which we crossed in safety, though we had to raise our wagon-beds in order to keep them dry. Day warm. Thunder and lightning, but no rain. The river makes a sudden bend south, and the trail leaves it and lies over a spur of the mountains, reaching it again in about eight miles. After going about four miles, we came to a long and difficult hill. In the valley east of it is a stream, which empties into Bear River within sight. Some of our company thought we could reach the river by sunset, but the first ascent being set at nought, their calculations were wrong. It was nearly sunset by the time we reached the summit, and here, without wood or water, our cattle being tired, and one having fallen dead in coming up, we determined to stop for the night. A party of us returned to the stream for water, to make coffee, etc.—a distance of about two miles. As we descended the mountain the mosquitoes commenced an assault upon us and General Taylor would have been compelled to surrender upon this occasion. I never before saw them half so numerous or so bloodthirsty. They stung my hands so much that they were soon badly swollen. After fighting them about half an hour, we were successful in getting back with a few quarts of water. Distance, twenty miles.

June 23.

This morning we drove four miles to Bear River and stopped for the day, all needing rest. A family of the Snake Indians came to our camp and asked for sugar and powder. They were dressed in dirty buckskin and looked very wretched. We see already upon the road numerous stragglers, men having lost their teams and provisions, and those who started unprepared. Our speed on the road has been much better than we expected. For more than a month we have seen the same companies, some of them supplied with the best teams. Distance, four miles.

June 24.

Started early this morning, all in good spirits. Continued down the valley but were not within several miles of the river for most of the day, and did not come close to it at all, though we crossed a great many streams, which came down from the range of mountains on our right, and emptied into Bear River. Though we had crossed many streams during the day, at night we camped not less than three miles from it. A couple of our men went to the river for some water, and when they returned they declared that it was not less than four miles to it. It appears about one mile and a half. Road today excellent. The wild sage which covered most of the country from Fort Laramie to Green River is not so prolific in this region, but a great many plants spring up among the grass, some of which bear beautiful blossoms. Distance, twenty-six miles.

June 25.

Went two miles to water and took breakfast; about eight miles farther we came to Cold Springs. They spring up out of the plain near the trail and make quite a respectable stream. The water is remarkably cold and good. Opposite the Cold Springs, and about a half a mile to the right, is another natural curiosity, called Beer Springs. These springs are so called from the fact that these springs have a sour taste, somewhat resembling beer. It springs out of an elevated, light-colored rock, which I suppose was caused by the petrification of certain properties in the water. Upon the center of the elevation are several sharp-pointed rocks, from which the water rushes. Several of these conical rocks, larger than the rest, are now exhausted. They must have been great curiosities when in full play. Four miles further on, and within two yards of Bear River, are Steamboat Springs. The water of these springs, which gushes from the rocks is warm, which is the more remarkable from the fact of its being so close to the river. Just beyond this place the Bear River bends suddenly round the mountains, to the south, and here we leave it. It is well known it rises in the great basin and empties into Salt Lake. A little to the west of the bend is the old crater, so called from the supposition that it was once a volcano, the base alone remaining. The rocks in this ruinous-looking place bear the marks of fire. Opposite to the old crater the road branches off to Fort Hall, the one we are traveling (Hedspeths [?] Cutoff), continuing west. Distance, twenty miles.

June 26.

This afternoon we crossed the vide that divides the waters of the Great Basin from those of the Pacific. This we know from the fact that we crossed a branch of the Pont Neuf River. At night we encamped by the Pont Neuf. It is from ten to fifteen yards wide, and deep. We saw some Snake Indians today. They have plenty of horses, which they offer to sell. The country before us appears very mountainous. I must cut today's note short, as it takes both hands to keep off the mosquitoes. Confound the mosquitoes! Distance, twenty miles.

June 27.

Today our road led over very mountainous country. We crossed two high mountain ranges, with a fine stream of water between them. In advance of us our path was filled up with mountains, one upon another. Snow to be seen. There are two classes of mountains in this region, the largest covered with snow and the smaller one having vegetation and filling up the space between the others. Upon the peaks of some of the highest mountains is a stunted growth of cedar, which gives them rather a dark appearance. I have often heard when at home that buffalo did not abound west of the south pass, but I have seen numerous evidences in the shape of skulls by the road; but it is said by the Indians that there are not at this time any buffalo in this region, nor has there been for six years past. A sufficient cause for their entire disappearance in this region I cannot fully understand. Distance, sixteen miles.

June 28.

Most excellent road today, and down hill all the way, except a circuitous narrow gorge in the mountains of about four miles in length, which we went through in the afternoon. In descending the western slope of this range we found the road very steep, though we came down in safety. At the soda springs we saw an old man who called himself Captain Grant. He assured us that one half of our cattle would die on the cut-off, for want of grass, and also that the road was almost impassable and no nearer than that by Fort Hall. This statement in respect to grass is utterly untrue, and we suspect the others are of like character. Grass on the cut-off is first rate—better than we have before seen on the road. Wild flax abounds in this region, though not in abundance. It is now in full bloom and looks quite like a flower garden in some places. We stopped by a little stream at noon, beyond which water is not so plenty for about twenty miles. There are willows growing along this stream. The road turns south after we cross it. We laid here until three o'clock and then went on about eight miles, passing over a range of low mountains, and encamped at night in the valley. A shower of rain in the afternoon. Distance, twenty miles.

June 29.

Went down the valley about four miles to where it turned west over the mountains, when we unyoked the cattle and drove them in a southeast direction to a spring of water. About eight miles more brought us to a valley in which were several good springs. In the afternoon went eight miles and found another spring of good water. Here we took in water for the night and encamped just beyond, where we found good grass. A little animal abounds in this region called the prairie squirrel. It is a little smaller than the common black squirrel, and gray in color. We see hundreds of them every day, and they are often killed with clubs and whips. I first noticed them in the vicinity of Fort Laramie, and have seen them every day since. The Indians, the Snakes principally, shoot them and use them as an article of food. Road good, weather pleasant. Distance, twenty miles.

June 30.

This morning we continued through the range of mountains which we entered yesterday. In the forenoon found plenty of water, passing several springs, and at length came to a mountain stream, which we followed down the valley. At noon we stopped opposite to a spur of rock. In the afternoon we struck out across the valley in a western direction. After crossing the stream which we followed in the morning, we went about twelve miles before we reached water. This stream was but four or five feet wide, but deep and difficult to cross. In this valley there is an abundant growth of wild sage and grease wood, but not much grass. Distance, twenty-seven miles.

July 1.

Went four miles this morning and came to what we supposed to be Raft River. It is about six yards wide and deep, like most of the other rivers in the mountains. We forded it and went up its valley about one mile and laid by till about 4 o'clock in the afternoon, when we proceeded three miles further and stopped for the night, the grass in which a heavy swath could be cut. Just after we crossed Raft River we came to the junction of the cut-off with the Fort Hall road. Those with whom we have spoken about the road represent it as being further and the worst of the two. On that road there are one or two very bad streams to cross, and also a mirey district. Distance, eight miles.

July 2.

Went up Raft River a short distance, when we crossed it and struck out in a southern direction. We went up a gentle slope for several miles and then descended into a wide valley, in which we crossed several streams and found plenty of grass. By one of these brooks we stopped at noon. In the afternoon we proceeded, and after going three miles, we entered the mountains again and went through a rugged region through the remainder of the day, though the road was good and water plenty. Towards evening we came to the junction of the Fort Hall and Salt Lake roads, about nineteen miles from where it crossed Raft River. We fell in with some emigrants direct from Salt Lake and got all the news we could. Provisions are represented as being very high there—flour $1.00 per pound and other things in proportion, except butter and milk, which are comparatively cheap. Distance, twenty-one miles.

July 3.

In the morning we went up Sleet (?) Creek, which we followed a mile or so up a ravine, and after descending the other side of the mountain, we reached what is called Goose Creek, a distance of about ten miles. This part of the day's drive was bad. In the afternoon we proceeded up Goose Creek about twelve miles. This stream is about six yards wide and the valley is narrow; grass good. Weather hot. Distance, twenty-two miles.

July 4.

The Fourth of July! What a glorious day, and how honored at home, but to the travel-worn emigrant, in the eternal wilds, this day's remembrances hardly stir the sluggish blood. All are rushing to the gold region, and few stop to celebrate the Fourth of July. We drove as usual, wild sage and dust being about the only thing in the eye. We followed up Goose Creek and a tributary for about ten miles, when we struck out across a high, dry country, destitute of vegetation, except wild sage, etc. After going twelve miles, we came to Thousand Spring Valley, and going down it a little more than a mile we found water and tolerable grass, where we stopped for the night. Day hot! Distance, twenty-three miles.

July 5.

Continued our march down the valley for ten miles, when we turned to the right, and on going two miles, came to what is called Dry Creek. In the afternoon we followed up this valley. In it there is the channel of a creek in which there is a little indifferent water in holes. A little farther on we noticed more water in the creek, and presently we saw it had increased to a stream. About ten miles up we stopped for the night, where we found a well of tolerable water. Grass first rate. Distance, twenty-two miles.

July 6.

We went up the valley this morning eight miles and crossed the stream which I suppose is called Cold Creek. Five miles more brought us to the end of the valley, where we found a good spring of water. In the afternoon we went over a range of mountains, and after going eight miles, came to another valley, in which we found a spring and good grass. Weather warm. Distance, twenty-one miles.

July 7.

Continued down the valley all day, except a few miles over a point of land running into a bend of the river. We found water in sloughs along the valley and at night came to a stream which is the head waters of Mary's or Humboldt's River. The valley is here broad and the grass good, though the soil is considerably impregnated with alkali. The weather cool and cloudy, with heavy rain seen falling upon the mountains in the afternoon. We begin to think that we have gained upon the great mass of emigrants, as we have not seen so many in the last few days; but this is owing to some extent by some having stopped at Salt Lake to recruit and others having gone by Fort Hall to Oregon. We at present overtake more than overtake us. Distance, twenty miles.

July 8.

This morning we reached the main stream of the long looked for Humboldt. The crossing was bad, the water being deep and the banks steep, though the stream is but about eight yards wide. The valley opens broad and affords a very extensive view of the country in advance of us. On our right rise the Humboldt Mountains, whose summits are covered with snow. The last rays of the setting sun are now lending to their spotless mantle a warm, rosy glow. One by one the lofty peaks lose their transient splendor, and outline after outline loses its distinctness in the sombre hues of evening. No timber in sight, except a little underbrush by the river. Today we passed a new-made grave, in which sleeps the last sleep of an emigrant who was shot a few days ago by an Indian, while on guard. Indians were about for the purpose of stealing horses and really did succeed in capturing one while the mounted guard was receiving the attention of the whole company. The fatal arrow was poisoned. This murder will raise great animosity against the Indians and the future emigrant, as he passes by the grave of his murdered countryman, will feel a spirit of revenge. The Root Diggers infest this region, a most savage and degraded tribe. Distance, twenty miles.

July 9.

Continued down the valley this morning some seven miles, when we came to a branch of the river and forded it. It is longer than the first we came to, though better to ford. At noon we met five men who had their team of six horses stolen last night by the Indians. There was but a single horse left among the five, and being unable to proceed with their effects, they were waiting for some fortunate opportunity. We put their provisions in with ours, intending to assist them through the journey, giving them equal advantages with ourselves. We take one of them in our wagon. This afternoon they found a written notice put up by the way, cautioning emigrants against the Indians, and stating that some twenty-five horses had been stolen by the Indians in that quarter within two or three days. They were taken in the night. A mule had been shot and a man captured and robbed. This will arouse new vigilance. We have not yet heard of any cattle being stolen. Distance, twenty-two miles.

July 10.

Nothing of note today. Continued down the valley thirteen miles by noon, then ascended a mountain and took a very circuitous course for the remainder of the day, making nine miles by night. Distance, twenty-two miles.

July 11.

Went down the Humboldt and crossed another stream, tributary to the former. After crossing it we commenced ascending a range of mountains and continued in this character of country for some fifteen or eighteen miles; but little water, and that in springs in the mountains. At night we reached the Humboldt again after having been from it some thirty-five miles. This portion of the road is new. The usual road is near the river, but could not be traveled now on account of high water. The face of the country is very barren, always excepting wild sage. Our road is very dusty. The dust is so light that the least wind raises it, though it does not impede the wheels of the wagons but little. Sometimes the dust is so heavy that we cannot see the wagon immediately ahead of us in the train. Quite a number of packers pass us daily. Provisions begin to get scarce. Constant applications are made. Distance, twenty-six miles.

July 12.

Having made a long drive yesterday, we rested today till noon. As we started we turned off to the right and reached the river again at the end of eight miles, continued along it a mile or two, crossed another low range of hills about two miles across, and camped for the night by the Humboldt, a short distance further on. Distance, twelve miles.

July 13.

Continued down the valley, which is very wide at this point. Toward night we entered into another bend of the river, running across by north and south. The general surface of the soil here is nearly bare, wild sage, greasewood and a few stunted weeds being the only vegetation. The soil is light in color and weight, and walking through it is like walking through ashes or slacked lime. Most of the day we were several miles from the river and came to it but twice during the day, I never saw such dense clouds of dust as I saw here, and it is more disagreeable on account of being impregnated with alkali, which abounds in this valley. The sky is cloudless and the sun extremely warm. We have traveled so long among the mountains, and all bearing the same general appearance, that we seem to be stationary instead of changing our position every day. In looking around me I seem to be in a deep blue ocean of air, with the distant mountains around as the shore. Distance, twenty-three miles.

July 14.

Went on this morning over a most desolate plain, with scarcely a vestige of vegetation, except greasewood. We traveled fifteen miles before we reached the river, and then found no grass on the east side; but as some men were ferrying grass across in a wagon bed, we procured it and brought over grass for our cattle. After going two miles further we came to a fork in the road, one running down the river and the other passing over a low range of bluffs. We followed the latter and came to the river again in about two miles. Distance, twenty miles.

July 15.

This morning we went on eight miles, when we came to the river, where we stopped to water.

Here we found quite a number of wagons which were stopped in consequence of a report that they were near the desert and at the place where it was necessary to take in grass. We made inquiries and examined our uncertain guides, which tended to corroborate the report. The indications were all affirmative, but the distance was too short. Several hundred wagons have gone directly off the road eight miles to procure grass for their stock on the desert, and finally we concluded to go also, and be on the safe side at any rate. In the afternoon we traveled to the grass and found it tolerably good and was enabled in the afternoon to cut as much as we could conveniently carry. Day hot. Distance, eight miles.

July 16.

Up and off early. Came to the river again some three miles below where we left it. A little lower down we stopped at noon. By the way, one of our men went on twelve miles yesterday noon to see if we were as near the sink as was supposed. We found the appearance of the river unchanged and concluded that the sink was not near. However, we determined to take on our grass and use it when necessary. In the afternoon we went over a low range of hills some six miles in distance, then we came to the river, and soon stopped for the night, and found good grass after a good deal of trouble in getting our oxen over a bad slough. Distance, twelve miles.

July 17.

In the forenoon we were thrown off our main course some three miles by having to go round a slough. We met some packers from California, who informed us that we were 140 miles from the sink. We discredited their statement, but soon after came to some emigrants who were old neighbors of these Californians and was told by them that confidence might be placed in the report. This disappointment came extremely hard to those who were nearly out of provisions. Some are already destitute of food and have to depend on the liberality of others. Some are killing their work cattle for beef. One man in our own company offered $10 for five pounds of flour and could not get it. The grass and water in this region are poor. Weather warm. Distance, eighteen miles.

July 18.

There being but little grass where we stopped last night, we went on this morning before breakfast about five miles. Being weary of the journey and wishing to proceed as fast as possible, I here sold out my share in the team, and in company with another of our party who sold out his team also, proceeded ahead of the wagons, carrying our provisions upon a pony, going in company with six others from the same company, who set out in consequence of being short of eatables. Most of the day we kept by the river, but just at night happened to get upon a sand plain of fifteen miles, without grass or water. We came upon this distance unawares and suffered much for water. About 9 o'clock we reached the river again, greatly fatigued. Distance, thirty-five miles.

July 19.

Proceeded down the river and went round a great bend to the north. Grass very scarce. Hot weather. A breeze every noon; soil very light. Distance, twenty-two miles.

July 20.

Light sand plain. River bottom narrow. No grass. Dead animals. Destruction of property. Distance, twenty-two miles.

July 21.

Fourteen miles to good spring—two to river—three to grass for the desert. Grass plenty. Beef twenty-five cents per pound. One hundred wagons preparing. Weather hot. Destitution of food among the emigrants. Distance, twenty-three miles.

July 22.

Started early for the sink. Country barren. Bad water. Distance, twelve miles.

July 23 and 24.

Crossed the desert forty miles. Eight miles to the sink. Went upon the desert at 4 o'clock P. M. Saw many dead animals. First part road level and good. Moonlight night. Wagons strewn along the road. Latter part of the road deep sand. Reached Carson River at 11 o'clock A. M. Saw timber for the first time in several hundred miles.

July 25.

Went up river twelve miles, then from it for fifteen miles over a high desert country. Valley of river narrow and well timbered. Distance, twenty-seven miles.

July 26.

Left the river and went twenty-six miles before we came near it again. Country barren and broken.

July 27.

Went up river eight miles, then left it for twelve. Road mountainous, with a little cedar. Distance, twenty miles.

July 28.

By river one mile, from it five, then up the valley remainder of the day. Valley wide—numerous mountain streams, fine grass and fine flowers. A high mountain on our right. Snow on some of the peaks. Nights cool. Past trading post. Provisions from a dollar to two dollars per pound. Packers and foot men rushing for the diggings. Distance, twenty-one miles.

July 29.

Up the valley twelve miles, then through a canyon six, then in camp two miles beyond; canyon rocky and ascending and full of timber. High mountains all around us. Distance, twenty miles.

July 30.

To dividing range of mountains, with Red Lake at foot, five miles. Over this range and down to another lake, six miles. Over Snow Mountain to Rock Valley, ten miles. (Through snow two miles.) Road over continual rocks; snow in places, and timber. Cool day and freezing at night. On the mountain, amid the melting snows, were flowers of the most brilliant colors, and the road passed for many miles among gigantic pines. Distance, twenty-one miles.

July 31.

Went fifteen miles to Leak [Leap (?)] Spring Valley. Country mountainous and well timbered.

August 1.

Went seventeen miles to the junction of the Weaver and Hangtown roads. No grass and but little water on the road in this distance. Road bad.

August 2.

Went seventeen miles to Pleasant Valley, in the vicinity of Ringgold and Weaver. Here the country begins to look like California—canvas houses, hot weather, dry, reddish soil. This day's travel I consider the conclusion of a journey, a longer or more tedious than which is not often performed on this earth.

"The heart rebounds with long forgotten fleetness" at the thought of having performed it. The interminable wastes are passed over, the wilderness of wild sage and ashes is behind me, and climbing a hundred mountains will no longer tire my feet. This act is ended, and now for a struggle for gold and then

"Oh! for a falcon's wing to bear, To bear me to my home."

NOTE.

The distances in the foregoing journal are probably inaccurate, as we had no means to measure them, and depended entirely on our own judgment. In reading it over, I have noticed many typographical and grammatical errors, but these will be excused when it is recollected that it was written for the most part in haste and at different times.

C. W. S.

Page 32 suceeded changed to succeeded Page 24 conditon changed to condition Page 13 nigh changed to night Page 6 wil changed to will Page 5 wonderings changed to wanderings

Typographical errors corrected in the text: Some inconsistent hyphenation and spelling in the original document has been preserved.

Transcriber's Note

Made in the USA
Columbia, SC
09 December 2021